THE AMERICAN INDIANS

of

AZEITA

"HIS PEOPLE"

INTRODUCTION BY JOSEPH STACEY
ARIZONA HIGHWAYS MAGAZINE

SPECIAL DEDICATION AND SONG BY
JOHNNY CASH, NASHVILLE, TENN.

A RICK TANNER PUBLICATION
P.O. BOX 302
SCOTTSDALE, ARIZONA 85252

Library of Congress Catalog Card No. 76-27119
Hardcover No. 76-27119

PRINTING HISTORY
First U.S. Edition: June, 1976
Hardcover Edition: July, 1976

Second U.S. Edition: September, 1976
Second U.S. Hardcover Edition: October, 1976

BOOK DESIGN AND TEXT BY RICK W. TANNER

LIMITED EDITION PRINTS — have been produced of
the cover painting, LIFE GOES ON and of several
other paintings featured in the following
pages. For information contact Rick Tanner
Publications, P.O. Box 302, Scottsdale,
Arizona 85252.

Jim Abeita Photograph by Peter Bloomer

OTHER RICK TANNER PUBLICATION BOOKS.

ACKNOWLEDGMENTS

Grateful acknowledgment is extended to the following for their help during
the two and one-half years this compilation was being prepared.

    To the artist himself, Jim Abeita, whose patience and generosity with
his time and talents made this project a beautiful reality. Jim, if it had not been
for your enthusiasm and most especially your trust and friendship, my dream
would not be in print today.

    Special acknowledgment and thanks go to Mr. and Mrs. Thomas R.
McLean for their interest and encouragement, but particularly the confidence
placed in me and the publication.

    To my family and especially Strawberry for their aid and understanding
in this project.

    To the Dandick Co. and Associated Lithographers of Phoenix, Arizona
for the incredible printing and remarkably perfect color reproduction and also
to Dick Millar for his knowledge, advice, and criticism.

    My deepest appreciation goes to the Johnny Cash family, whose en-
couragement and love was given to Jim and his children when it was needed
most. Our visits enabled me to witness a man's beliefs, share in his family har-
mony and see his love for fellow man and his country. To me Johnny Cash is
truly an American's American.

                                                            Rick W. Tanner

Cover Painting

LIFE GOES ON — 36x48 oil. Private collection. "Life Goes On" was
painted by Jim Abeita after the death of his wife, Hannah. The spirit of
continuity with their cultural background and the strength Jim obtains from
his ancestral homelands is depicted here in the nobility of the procession
as Abeita and his friends come riding out of the canyons bordered by cliffs
in Navajo country.

Title Page Painting

NATURES CARVINGS — 3x16 oil. Collection of Mr. and Mrs. Ellis Tanner,
Gallup, NM.

Inside Back Cover Painting

WINTER GRAZING — 24x36 oil. Private collection.

Back Cover Painting

THE GRAND PRIZE BELT — 18x24 oil. Collection of Tanners Indian Arts,
Scottsdale, Arizona. Painted especially for Arizona Highways, to use as the
back cover of the 1974 August issue.

INTRODUCTION

This magnificent book is about an artist, his family and friends; their ways of life and the beauty of their land. Jim Abeita is a fine artist. He is a full-blooded Navajo Indian who paints pure pictorial documentaries created from his own first hand knowledge of his subject, portrayed so vividly and accurately that we must qualify Jim Abeita as a reliable historian.

Jim Abeita's paintings hold no mystical or hidden messages. No need to ask: what is this artist trying to tell me—about his emotions—about life—about himself? Is he succeeding in telling me his story—do I understand what he is trying to tell me—and why? No mental challenges or sensual fatigue with Jim Abeita's paintings because his art is pure and absolute realism. He paints everything he sees—as he sees it—easily and naturally. The more we see of Jim and his art the more we believe he comes closest to being a "born natural" artist than anyone we know.

Our first exposure to the art of Jim Abeita was at the 1972 All Indian Inter-Tribal Ceremonials, Gallup, New Mexico. His painting, "Navajo Peyotism," was the Grand Prize award winner, (page 31). It was the first time the young Navajo artist had exhibited in a competitive show. We met Jim Abeita, for the first time, two years later, at the 1974 Tanner's All-Indian Invitational show, Scottsdale, Arizona, where his paintings were awarded top honors. "Last Minute Polish," (page 37), received the Grand Prize of the show, it was at this time I decided to use it for the cover painting of the 1974 August issue of Arizona Highways Magazine.

Today, in May of 1976, it is difficult for us to realize that the quiet, serene-souled, soft-voiced young Indian we met in '74 is the source for the genius and drive represented in the superb color reproductions of this book. We don't usually use the word "genius" loosely. In this case the genius of our young Indian friend is reflected from every page.

At 28, Jim Abeita has mastered his technique. His genius goes far beyond the limits of mere technique. Here genius indicates a perfection of technique—plus something else—the artist's native temperament, to feel as a Navajo, with the inborn, instinctive sensitivity to feel *about* their ways and their environment; both apart from and unlike the rest of humanity and the geography of this planet.

Jim Abeita admits his marked racial temperament and maintains strongly its identity and validity. He enters into the world of his people, their ways and places with the same sense that they enter into him. No other Indian artist paints Navajo people, horses and action like Jim Abeita. There have been some great names in the roll of Navajo artists: Harrison Begay, Quincy Tahoma, Gerald Nailor, Andy Tsinhnahjinnie, Beatien Yazz, Tony Begay, all especially noted for their traditional poetic portrayals of the Navajo and his "beautyways." Adee Dodge, one of the most prolific Navajo artists is collected for his spirit horses and fastidiously drawn interpretations of Navajo myths and legends. Internationally acclaimed Navajo contemporary, R.C. Gorman, wants but a faint recollection of reservation days and ways as he continues to please a sophisticated clientele using non-Indian techniques.

Jim Abeita's art is distinctively distinguished by accurate and meticulous rendering of detail. Everything is clearly defined and stated.

In the general overall universe of art, Indian art is as a galaxy of newly discovered stars, undefinable to many experts, but undeniably coming through the haze of categories, definitions, and establishment boundaries as influenced by geographical, ethnic and social-political backgrounds.

We believe that art basically lives and dies in but two categoric divisions—"good art" and "bad art." The art of Jim Abeita is good art executed to the superlative degree of Indian, Navajo, Western and American art standards.

We don't know of many artists with steam enough to go at full throttle for a lifetime. Jim Abeita has come a long way since 1972 and we honestly believe he has what it takes to go all the way to the apex of greatness in his chosen field. At 28 he is certainly blessed with a better-than-average touch of greatness, sometimes translated by non-Indians as divine inspiration, no mean birthday gift in itself. Either you haven't got it, or you haven't learned to manage it, or it works only under special conditions, or for some obscure emotional or physical reason your nervous mechanism will not carry a charge of sufficient intensity to command attention.

Jim Abeita's art is "off the pad" and into a dominant attention-compelling orbit. The reproductions especially selected for this book are only part of Jim Abeita's five-year artistic output. They speak most eloquently for Jim Abeita, the Indian people, and their wonderful, wonderfilled land.

Joseph Stacey

NAVAJO
By Johnny Cash

I have seen your colors woven in your blankets
I have heard your names on rivers and on towns
I have seen your turquoise on fine, fancy ladies
The Indian sun is rising instead of goin' down.

    Navajo, Navajo
    The people call the people from
       ten thousand years ago
    Navajo, Navajo
    From the land of the enchantment,
       Navajo.

I have seen your red rock canyons out of Gallup
I've walked upon your Arizona hills
At Crown Point I watched an artist painting
The secrets of your past surviving still.

I've seen your women dressed in royal purple
The silver from your hills upon their hands
And I need no signpost reading reservation
To know the minute I'm on Indian land.

JIMMY ABEITA

I have been writing songs for about twenty-one years professionally and often times I am asked "Where did you get the idea for that song?" Song ideas come different ways. I'll hear a phrase that will trigger an idea or I'll see something or someone, I'll remember something even, that will give me an idea for a song. But a rich source of inspiration is other people. Jimmy Abeita has been one of those people to me.

I've known Jimmy for several years now. He and his family have been guests in my home on numerous occasions. I've come to know him as a man that I greatly admire and respect. In the years that I have traveled this country on concert tours I've been on many Indian reservations. I've spoken with various Indian peoples, I've listened to the militant and I've sat and talked with the old men about ancient customs. One of the most inspiring people that I have ever known is Jimmy Abeita. I respect him for what he is, what he does and what he is trying to do. I know that in his heart, the mark he wants to leave in this world is to paint a picture of the culture, of the character, of the humanity of his People. The night after I visited him on the reservation at Crown Point, New Mexico, I wrote a song which he inspired. The song is called NAVAJO, and though the song is about the Navajo people in general, Jimmy Abeita is really that one special Navajo in the song. May his works inspire you as he, himself, has inspired me.

Johnny Cash

HANNAH — 18x24 oil. Private collection.

Hannah Foster Abeita, June 21, 1949-July 12, 1975.
Hannah was born in a Navajo hogan on the reservation in
Sheep Springs, NM. Hannah first met Jim during his senior
year of high school at Gallup, NM. After graduation they were
married and with the help of the Navajo Tribe, they moved
to Chicago so Jim could study for two years at the American
Academy of Art.

Jim has always said without the help and love of
Hannah he would have never succeeded in his goals. She
blessed him with three lovely children, Michelle, Troy, and
Carma. Hannah was a beautiful companion, and loving wife,
for which she will be fondly missed and compassionately
thought of and remembered.

IN DEDICATION TO
HANNAH ABEITA

whose smiling face shines through the grief of our loss, this book is lovingly
and respectfully dedicated. For this was one of Hannah's dreams, that some-
day there would be a book of her husband Jimmy's works.

Behind every great man you will always find a great woman and we'll
always remember Hannah as that woman and as the devoted wife and mother
who believed in, encouraged, and aided her husband in reaching his goals.

John Cash

Top) GRAND CANYON—
24 x 48 oil. Collection of Mr.
and Mrs. Thomas R. McLean,
Santa Ana, CA.

Bottom) WEAVERS IMAGE—
16 x 20 oil. Private collection,
Gallup, NM.

Left) CANYON DE CHELLY—
24 x 36 oil. Collection of Mr.
and Mrs. Manual Chavez,
Huntington Beach, CA.

Top) PAWN! — 8 x 10 oil. Private collection.

Bottom) SANDPAINTING CEREMONY — 24 x 36 oil. Collection of Mr. and Mrs. Beasley, Albuquerque, NM.

Right) AMERICAN HERITAGE — 24 x 30 oil. Collection of Mr. and Mrs. Thomas R. McLean, Santa Ana, CA. Awarded Grand Prize at the annual, Tanner's All Indian Invitational Pottery and Painting Show, 1976, Scottsdale, Arizona. Chosen to be used in Arizona Highways bicentennial issue, July 1976.

Top) ZUNI OLYA MAIDENS — 24 x 48 oil. Collection of Mr. and Mrs. Charles Kauzlarich, Gallup, NM. Grand Prize award winning painting at the 1973 Gallup Inter-Tribal Indian Ceremonial; Gallup, NM.

Bottom) FANCY RUFFLE DANCER — 16 x 20 oil. Private collection.

Left) YEI'S — 32 x 44 oil. Collection of Advertising Unlimited, Mankato, MN. Popularity award winning painting at the 1973 Tanner's Annual All Indian Invitational Pottery and Painting Show, Scottsdale, Arizona.

Top) LISA — 8 x 10 oil. Collection of
the artist.

Bottom) SELF-PORTRAIT — 18 x 24 oil.
Collection of the artist.

Left) CHRISTIE — 16 x 20 oil. Collection
of Dr. and Mrs. Jack L. Adams,
Albuquerque, NM.

Top) TURQUOISE LADY — 18 x 24 oil. Collection of Mr. and Mrs. A. R. Black, Albuquerque, NM.

Bottom) FIRST BORN — 24 x 36 oil. Collection of the artist.

Left) MUST OF LOST HIS HOBBLE — 24 x 36 oil. Collection of Ed Grose and Associates, Scottsdale, Arizona. Traditionally Navajo families would hobble their horses to graze freely on the unfenced reservation land.

THE WINNERS — 24 x 36 oils, private collection, Scottsdale, Arizona. Abeita, commissioned by Rick Tanner to paint a group portrait of his annual Tanner's All Invitational Winners, discovered that he too was a winner! 1974 portrait (above), top row includes contemporary potter Tony Da, Santa Clara potter Joseph Lonewolf and Navajo jewelry artist Lee A. Yazzie all of whom were winners again in 1975 Tanner competition. In the next row Abeita caught the spirit of Hopi kachina doll carver and painter, Silas Roy. Next to him is Helen Hardin whose abstract paintings in acrylic reflect traditional symbols. Helen's mother is the celebrated Santa Clara painter, Pablita Velarde. Also in the third row is Preston Monongye whose Hopi jewelry put him in the Winners portrait in 1975 again, along with Abeita whose self-portrait is in the lower left hand corner.

For the 1975 Tanner's All Invitational Winners group portrait (right), Abeita incorporated the heritage and reflected the art abilities of the individual winners, blending their cultural motifs in a rich mosaic background which gives drama to the painting.

Circled about Tony Da, an inventive artist who adapts heritage from his San Ildefonso Grandmother, Maria, to accommodate inlays of heshi and turquoise in his contemporary pottery are two more repeat winners, Preston Monongye the Hopi jewelry artist and Lee A. Yazzie, the Navajo jewelry artist noted for his lapidary skill with turquoise. Valjean Hessing, Choctaw artist who does her superb opaque watercolors based on ancestral lore is in the right hand corner. Abeita winner again and painter of the group portrait appears in the left hand corner with the portrait of Joseph Lonewolf just above him. Lonewolf's incised pottery "jewels" whose designs come to him from a centuries old Santa Clara culture completes the 1975 winners circle. The Winners Show is held annually in Scottsdale, Arizona. For information contact Rick Tanner.

Top) WINDOW ROCK — 30 x 40 oil. Artist collection. Each year the Navajo Tribal Government at Window Rock near the Arizona-New Mexico border, holds an annual Navajo Tribal Fair, an event recognized for its superior exhibits of American Indian art and pageantry. The painting "Window Rock" was created by Jim Abeita for the book cover for this annual Fair in 1974. Here Abeita presents what he imagined the first Tribal Fair was like, portraying people, horses and wagons gathered to chat and share their art, to sing and dance, brought together by a mutual cultural inheritance. In the background is the "window" in the sandstone cliffs eroded by centuries of swirling wind and sand.

Bottom) MONTEZUMA'S CASTLE — 16 x 20 oil. Private collection, Scottsdale, Arizona.

Left) HÁTAHĹEY — 24 x 36 oil. Private collection, Scottsdale, Arizona. Title is Navajo for, Medicine Man, head singer.

AUGUST SNOW — 10 x 14 oil.
Private collection.

MILES AND MILES — 16 x 20 oil.
Private collection.

NOT FOR SALE — 16 x 20 oil.
Private collection.

THE ABEITA CHILDREN — Easily the artist's favorite
subject matter. 12 x 14 oils, private collection.

Top) CHARLES LOLOMA — 16 x 20 oil. Private
collection. Jim Abeita created this pre-
liminary study of Charles Loloma, internationally known Hopi contemporary
jewelry artist for the cover of a forthcoming
Rick Tanner Publication book on artists,
their hallmarks and techniques entitled,
"The Finest of American Indian Jewelers."

Bottom) SPRING TIME — 10 x 14 oil. Private
collection.

Top) YEIBICHAI — 24 x 48 oil. Private collection.
The Night Chant or Night Way — more
commonly referred to as the Yeibichai.
Abeita's painting depicts the yeis out
collecting food and pollen to be used in
the ceremony.

Bottom) HER WEALTH — 14 x 14 oil. Collection of
Dr. and Mrs. George Breon, La Jolla, CA.

Opposite CONCERN, FOR TRIBAL AFFAIRS —
page) 24 x 36 oil. Collection of Mr. and Mrs. Rick
W. Tanner, Scottsdale, Arizona.

Top) HAPPIEST— 16 x 20 oil. Collection of Mr. and
Mrs. Bruce Williams, Gallup, NM.

Bottom) PACKIN' TO LOW COUNTRY— 24 x 36 oil.
Private collection.

Left) TWO GENERATIONS— 16 x 20 oil.
Collection of Mr. and Mrs. Rod Rindels,
Albuquerque, NM.

GRANDPARENTS—24 x 30 oil. Collection of
Dr. and Mrs. Walter K. Grigg, Phoenix, Arizona.

SMILE OF ALL INDIAN DAYS—16 x 20 oil.
Private collection, Gallup, NM.

NAVAJO PEYOTISM — 16 x 20 oil. Private collection. Grand prize award winning
painting at the 1972 Gallup Inter-Tribal Indian Ceremonial, Gallup, NM.

Top) RESERVATION DUST— 18 x 24 oil. Private collection, Scottsdale, Arizona.

Bottom) CHEYENNE WARRIOR— 8 x 10 oil. Collection of Mr. and Mrs. William G. Mennen, Scottsdale, Arizona.

Right) HIS PEOPLE— 30 x 40 oil. Collection of Mr. and Mrs. Joe E. Tanner, Gallup, NM. A Portrait of some of the members of the artist family. Featured in the 1974 October issue of Arizona Highways Magazine.

Top) STEPHANIE—
24 x 48 oil.
Private collection.

Bottom) ZUNI CLUSTER—
16 x 20 oil.
Private collection.

Left) RAINBOW—
16 x 20 oil. Collection
of Mr. & Mrs. Ed Ross,
Phoenix, Arizona.

Top) TSOSIE — 16 x 20 oil. Private collection.

Bottom) FAITH AND HOPE — 18 x 24 oil. Collection of Mr. and Mrs. Virgil Gerig, Sedona, Arizona. Inside cover illustration of the 1974 Christmas issue of Arizona Highways Magazine.

Right) LAST MINUTE POLISH — 24 x 30 oil. Collection of Mr. and Mrs. Russ Lyon, Sr., Scottsdale, Arizona. Grand Prize award winning painting at the 1974 Tanner's Annual All Indian Invitational Pottery and Painting show, Scottsdale, Arizona. Used as the front cover illustration of the 1974 August issue of Arizona Highways Magazine.

Top) CAMILIO — 12 x 16 watercolor. Private collection. The first painting Jim Abeita created after the death of Hannah was this splendid watercolor portrait of Camilio Sunflower Tafoya, the oldest, active male potter in the Southwest and respected tribal leader. Camilio who for many years produced the traditional black Santa Clara pottery now does red pottery with incised designs. His daughter, Grace Medicine Flower, and his son, Joseph Lonewolf, have inherited their Father's skills with clay making, shaping, and coloring. They too create pots of exceptional quality and beauty inspired by symbols from Nature and from their ancestral culture for use in their incised pottery.

Bottom) SERENITY — 9 x 18 watercolor. Private collection, Scottsdale, Arizona.

AFTERNOON — 10 x 14 watercolor.
Private collection.

GOT-YA — 14 x 18 watercolor.
Collection of Mr. and Mrs.
Daniel S. May, Jackson Hole, WY.

SIX, GOING ON OLD — 10 x 10 Watercolor.
Collection of Billy Price, Scottsdale, Arizona

Top) RAIN'Y DAY WOMAN — 6x9 oil.
Private collection, Gallup, NM.

Bottom) BREAKING CAMP — 24x36 oil.
Private collection, Scottsdale, Arizona.

Opposite WASTED DAYS — 24x36 oil.
page) Private collection.

Top) STUDY OF HANDS — 24 x 30 oil.
Private collection.

Bottom) SEEN WARMER DAYS — 24 x 36 oil.
Collection of Mr. and Mrs. Bob Eagle,
Dallas, Texas.

Opposite LEGEND OF THE TWINS — 24 x 36 oil.
page) Collection of Mr. and Mrs. Andy M.
Vigil, Albuquerque. Universal truth
that Man makes his own choice between
Good and Evil is message of old Indian
story-teller in Abeita's painting, "Legend
of the Twins."

WATER — 12 x 16 oil.
Private collection.

GOLDEN AUTUMN — 16 x 20 oil.
Private collection, Denver, Colorado.

CEREMONIAL DAY — 16 x 20 oil. Collection of
Mr. Lyle B. Underdown, Phoenix, Arizona.

MEDICINE MAN — 16 x 20 oil. Private
collection, Albuquerque, NM.

YAZZIE — 12 x 24 oil.
Private collection.

FINISHING TOUCH — 18 x 24 oil. Collection of Mr. and Mrs.
Manuel Chavez, Huntington Beach, CA.

TWEETER (YVONNIE)— 16 x 20 oil.
Artist collection.

SENTINEL — 18 x 24 oil. Collection of the Dandick Co., Scottsdale, Arizona.
Cover illustration of the New Mexico, Dandick Travel Tips.

TWENTY THREE MILES OR A DAY AND A HALF—
24 x 36 oil. Private collection.

MID-DAY WATER HOLE—24 x 30 oil. Collection of
Mr. and Mrs. N. T. Guadagnoli, Gallup, NM.

Four years ago in Chicago, Jim Abeita met Johnny Cash who was very impressed with a portrait Jim painted of him. At Johnny's request Jim and Hannah and children went to Nashville for several months to do some commissioned portraits and album covers. During this visit the two families developed a warm friendship.

When asked by Rick Tanner to write a profile of Jim Abeita for this book, Johnny Cash was also inspired to write a song about the Navajo culture, its strength and beauty which he had seen reflected in the life of Abeita. Then after Hannah's sudden death, Cash also wrote "A Dedication to Hannah" for the book which Cash knew meant so much to both Hannah and Jim.

The Jesus portrait and the painting below of John Carter and Gibbs are two of the Johnny Cash collection.

Opposite ZUNI PUEBLO LEADER —
page) 17 x 29 oil. Private collection.

JANUARY STORM — 24 x 36 oil. Private collection.

BUFFALO HUNT — 24 x 48 oil. Collection of Advertising Unlimited,
Mankato, MN.

PARADES, PARADES — 16 x 20 oil. Private collection.

Above) COUNCILMAN — 10x14 oil. Private
collection.

Right) INDIAN POWER — 16x20 oil. Collection
of Mr. and Mrs. Walter H. Hill, Jr., Tucson,
Arizona.

PROTECTION COMMITTEE— 36 x 48 oil. Private collection. Abeita's painting captures a group
of Navajo riders delivering the ceremonial staff used in the Squaw Dance. Traditionally the Entah or
Enemy Way-more commonly referred to as a Squaw Dance by non-Navajo was a war ceremonial
given to their warriors who had been contaminated by contact with the Enemy Today it's performed
for the need of the patient's diagnosed illness.

APACHE WARRIOR—
16x20 oil. Private collection.

Top) THUNDERHEAD — 12 x 16 oil.
Private collection.

Bottom) MONUMENT VALLEY —
24 x 48 oil. Collection of Mr. and
Mrs. James F. Lewis, Jr.,
Charlottesville, Virginia.

Opposite NILTÓLI′ TÓ′ — 24 x 36 oil. Private
page) collection. Title is Navajo for
transparent or clear water.

Top) PINON PICKERS — 24 x 30 oil. Collection of Mr. and Mrs. Thomas R. McLean, Santa Ana, California.

Bottom left) CLOUDY — 9 x 14 oil. Private collection.

Bottom right) STUDY OF HORSES — 16 x 20 oil. Collection of Mr. and Mrs. Hugh Williams, Gallup, NM.

CHARLIE GOODLUCK—
16x20 oil. Private collection.

Top) GOD BLESS AMERICA—
16x20 oil. Private collection.

Bottom) COLLECTING YUCCA—
18x24 oil. Private collection.

Left) NIZHÓNÍ HÓZHÓNÍ—
16x20 oil. Collection of
the Dandick Co. Title is
Navajo for beautiful.

CRISP, COLD DAY AT THE CANYON —
16 x 20 oil. Private collection.

TAOS DRUMMER — 10x14 oil
Private collection.

WARRIOR IN THE GRASS — 16 x 20 oil.
Artist collection.

ME TOO PLEASE — 8 x 10 oil.
Private collection, Phoenix, Arizona.

Top) CEREMONIAL LEADER
—8 x 10 oil. Private
collection, Scottsdale,
Arizona.

Bottom) MARKET DRIVE—
24 x 36 oil. Collection of
Mr. and Mrs. Ken Johns,
Albuquerque, NM.

Opposite PACKIN' IN—24 x 30 oil.
page) Private collection, Denver,
Colorado.

Top) SQUAW DANCE—24 x 36 oil. Collection
of Desses Sawyer, Tatum, NM. In this
painting Abeita shows the activity of
the third morning of the squaw dance.
During this time the people who gave
the dance for the patient receive gifts.

Bottom) FOUR SCORE AND SIXTEEN—
7 x 14 watercolor. Collection of Mr. and
Mrs. Rick W. Tanner, Scottsdale, Arizona.

Left) BLOOD HAWK—24 x 36 oil. Collection
of Tony Da, San Ildefonso, Pueblo, NM.

Top) WALPI — 24 x 36 oil.
Collection of Mr. and Mrs.
Rick W. Tanner, Scottsdale,
Arizona.

Bottom) VISION OF THE PAST —
8 x 10 oil. Artist collection.
Painted in the memory of the
late Tony Begay.

Opposite LATE START — 32 x 40 oil.
page) Private collection, Gallup, NM.

MAY THERE BE ENOUGH FOR ALL — 24 x 36 oil. Collection
of Mr. and Mrs. Joe E. Tanner, Gallup, NM.

SUMMER ENCAMPMENT — 18 x 36 oil. Collection of
Mr. and Mrs. Thomas R. McLean, Santa Ana, California.

PEYOTE CEREMONY — 18 x 24 oil. Collection of
Mr. and Mrs. W. A. Gerdts, San Diego, CA.

ABEITA MEDITATES

What will become of me?
Once I walked so tall
I won every prize in sight
I did it right
With Hannah I couldn't fall
What became of love?
Oh God, I miss her so
She was what I lived for
Now it seems a million moons ago
What will become of me?
Now my heart is cold
I painted life in these two hands
I had such plans
Now suddenly I feel old
My people have been good to me
And I can't let them down
The struggle goes on everyday
Dear God, let me pick up the pieces
Hannah would have wanted it that way

—Jean Flood